Teacher Created Resources

Listen · Read · Think

SCIENCE

What's in the Sky?

Ian Smith

Teacher Created Resources

Published in the United States by
QEB Publishing, Inc.
23062 La Cadena Drive
Laguna Hills
Irvine
CA 92653

This edition published by
Teacher Created Resources, Inc.
6421 Industry Way
Westminster, CA 92683
www.teachercreated.com

Library of Congress Control Number 2004102036

ISBN 978-1-4206-8147-5

Written by Ian Smith
Designed by Zeta Jones
Editor Hannah Ray
Picture Researcher Joanne Beardwell
Illustrated by Chris Davidson

Series Consultant Anne Faundez
Creative Director Louise Morley
Editorial Manager Jean Coppendale

Printed and bound in China
Picture credits

Key: t = top, b = bottom, m = middle, c = center, l = left, r = right

NASA/20b, 21b, 22m;
Corbis/Raymon Gehman 4 /Dennis Scott 20t;
Getty Imagés/Steve Bloom 15.

Contents

The Sun

Imagine a campfire so hot that you could warm your hands on it while standing on the other side of the street.

Now imagine something so hot that it warms your hands from MILLIONS of miles away! That's how hot the Sun is to us on Earth.

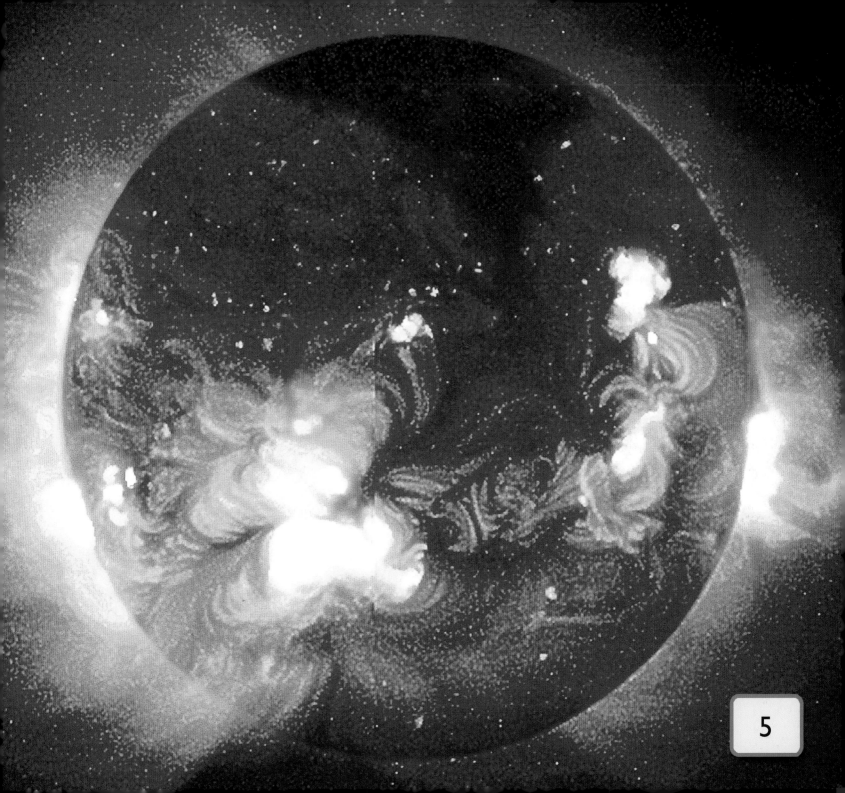

The Earth

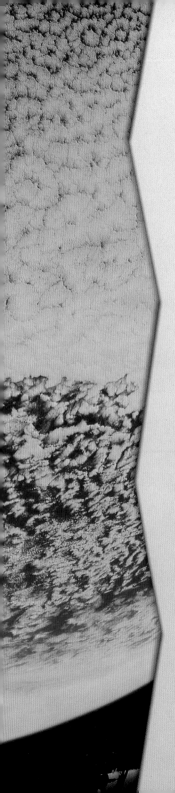

To an **astronaut** looking down from space, our Earth looks like a huge ball.

The Earth spins around all the time, like a giant top. It takes a day and a night to spin the whole way around.

Day and night

The side of the Earth that faces the Sun has daytime. The side that turns away from the Sun has nighttime.

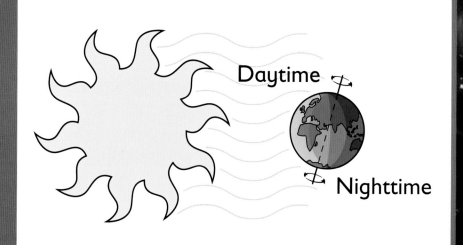

Daytime

Nighttime

As it spins, the Earth also travels around the Sun. The Earth takes a year to move all the way around the Sun. That's from one birthday to the next!

9

Weather

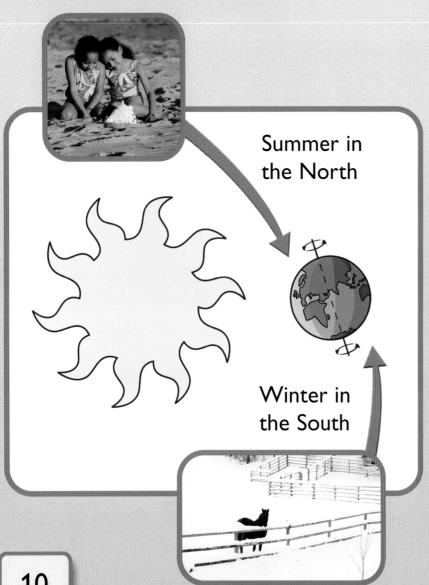

Summer in the North

Winter in the South

The part of the Earth that is leaning towards the Sun has warm weather.

The part of the Earth that is leaning away from the Sun has cold weather.

That's why it's cold in winter and hot in summer.

Winter in
the North

Summer in
the South

When it is winter in one part of the Earth, it is summer in another.

While children in the United States are enjoying the snow, in Australia they are cooling off on the beach!

The Earth seen
from the surface
of the Moon.

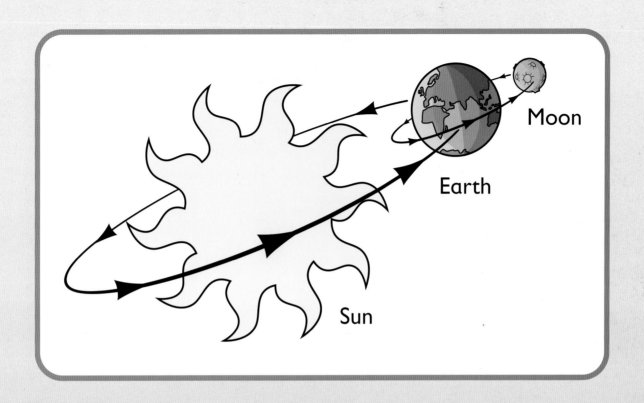

Moon

Earth

Sun

The sky is a very busy place! As the Earth moves slowly around the Sun, the Moon moves around the Earth. But it goes much faster. It takes the Moon only about a month to go all the way around the Earth.

The Moon has no heat or light of its own. It **reflects** the light of the Sun.

14

New Moon

Full Moon

A "New Moon" is nearly all in shadow.

A "Full Moon" is almost entirely lit up by the Sun.

The Moon seems to be a different shape each night that you look at it.

The Stars

What else do you see when you look up into the sky at night? You can see lots of stars twinkling.

These stars are very far away from us. They are even farther away from us than the Sun. That's why they look so small and don't seem as bright as the Sun.

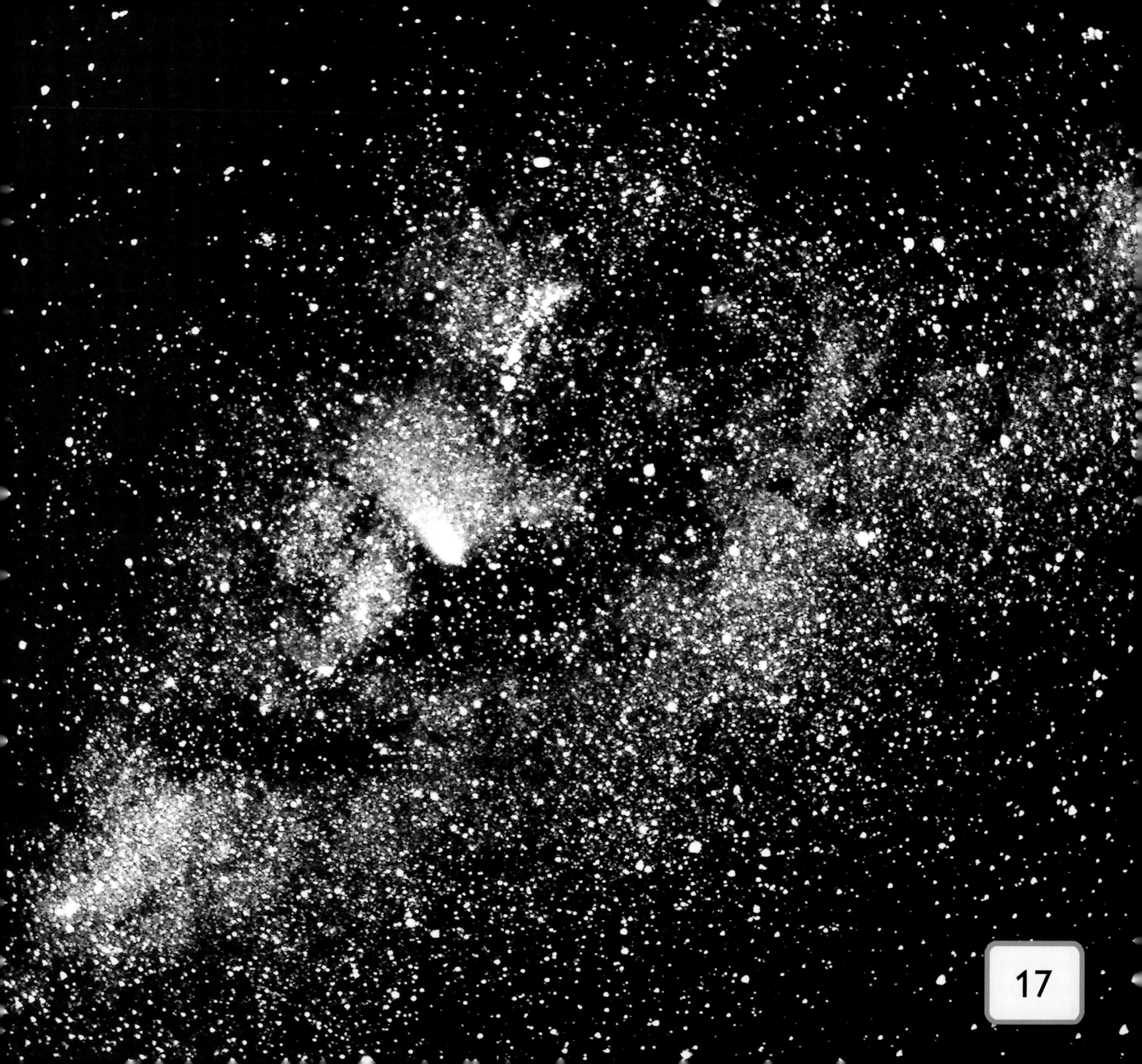

The Planets

Some of the brightest lights that we can see in the sky at night are called planets. The Earth is a planet, and there are seven other planets and one dwarf planet called Pluto. The other planets are called Mercury, Venus, Mars, Jupiter, Saturn, Uranus, and Neptune. All the planets move around the Sun.

Jupiter

Earth

Mars

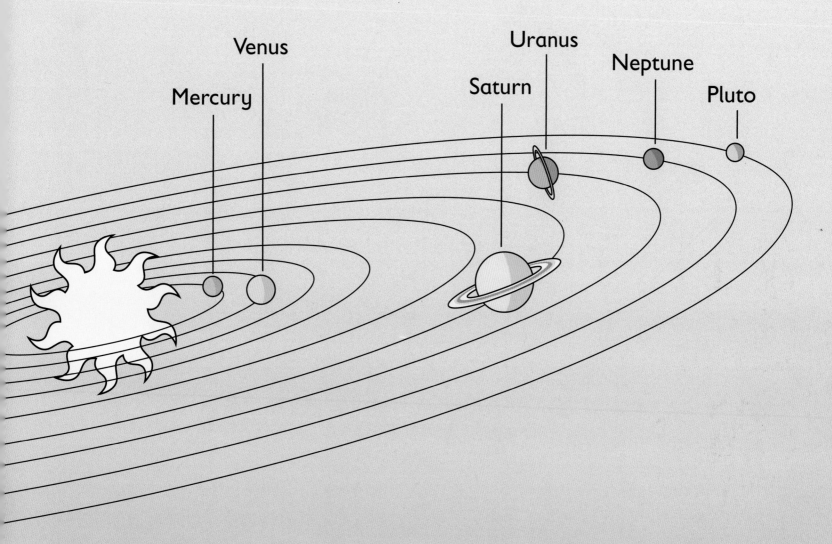

Mercury Venus Saturn Uranus Neptune Pluto

Astronomers are also discovering more and more planet-like objects called **planetoids**. Some of the planetoids are even farther from the Sun than Pluto.

The planets that are nearest the Sun are Mercury, Venus, Earth, and Mars.

Mercury is the closest planet to the Sun and takes only 88 days to go around it.

Mercury

Jupiter

Jupiter, Saturn, Uranus, and Neptune are very far away from the Sun. They circle the Sun very slowly.

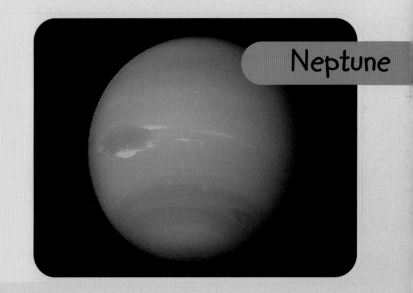

Neptune

If you lived on Neptune, you would have to wait 165 years for your birthday to come around!

Glossary

astronaut—a person who travels to space inside a spacecraft

astronomer—a person who studies space, including the Sun, Moon, stars, and planets

planetoid—a planet-like object, smaller than the eight main planets in our solar system

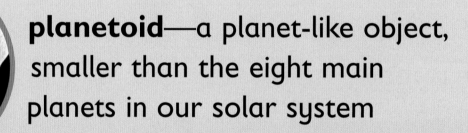

reflect—when light bounces off a surface

Index

astronaut 7, 22
astronomers 19, 22

daytime 8

Earth 6–8, 10, 11

Full Moon 15

Jupiter 18, 21

Mars 18, 20

Mercury 18, 20
Moon 12–15

Neptune 18, 21
New Moon 15

nighttime 8

planetoids 19, 22
planets 18–21
Pluto 18–19, 21

reflect 14, 22

Saturn 18, 21
stars 16–17
summer 10, 11
Sun 4–5, 8, 10, 14, 18, 19

Uranus 18, 21

Venus 18, 20

weather 10–11
winter 10–11

Parents' and teachers' notes

- Explain to your child that this book is nonfiction (it provides facts and information rather than telling a story) and that it contains a contents page (page 3), a glossary (page 22), and an index (page 23).
- Explain that by looking at the contents page, the reader can see what the book is about and the order in which the information appears in the book.
- Point out that the index is arranged alphabetically and can be used to locate specific information in the book.
- Explain that the glossary, also in alphabetical order, gives meanings for difficult or important words in the text.
- Re-read pages 4–5. Talk with your child about things that are hot and things that are cold. Use a hair dryer or some other heat source to show how quickly you lose the heat as you move away.
- Warn your child never to look directly at the sun as it can damage his/her eyes.

- Use a ball to show how the Earth moves slowly around on its axis.
- Encourage your child to look at the Moon each night to see its different stages.
- Together, sing "Twinkle, Twinkle Little Star."
- Count the planets in the diagram on pages 18–19. Repeat the names of the planets until your child is familiar with them. To help remember the names of the planets and their order from the Sun, make up a mnemonic, for example: **M**y **V**ery **E**arly **M**orning **J**ust **S**tarted **U**p **N**icely.
- Together, use reference books or the Internet to find out a fact about each of the planets. Help your child to write down his/her facts.
- Help your child write a fact sheet for an alien who wants to come and visit Earth, explaining all about the planet. Encourage your child to draw pictures to accompany his/her text. Can your child draw the alien, too?